M000091986

We are Vets

by Lada Josefa Kratky

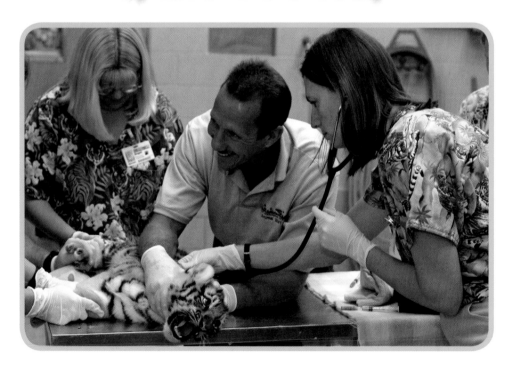

NATIONAL GEOGRAPHIC

School Publishing

We are vets. Come
and see what we do.

He is with the mom
and the cub.

We like the cubs to get big. They are fed a lot. See what they like?

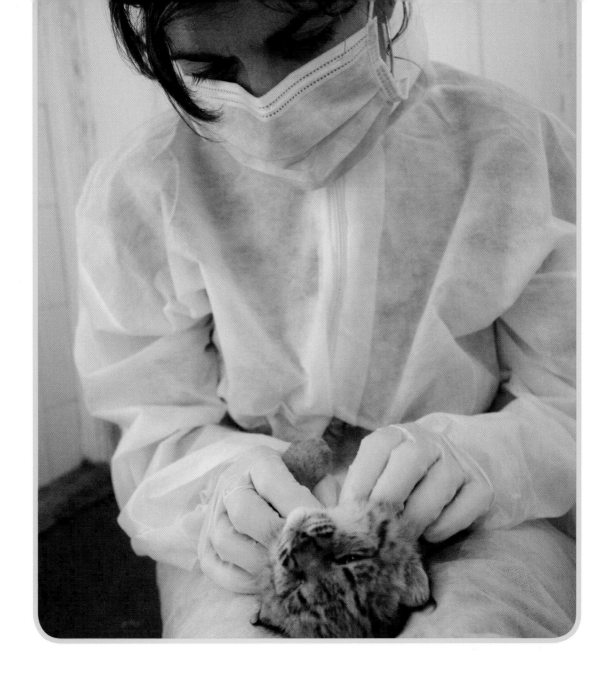

This cub can get a rub.
The vet can rub the cub.

Cubs like to have fun.
We can put a cub in a tub.
Look at this wet cub.

See how these cubs
have fun in the sun.
Rub a dub dub!

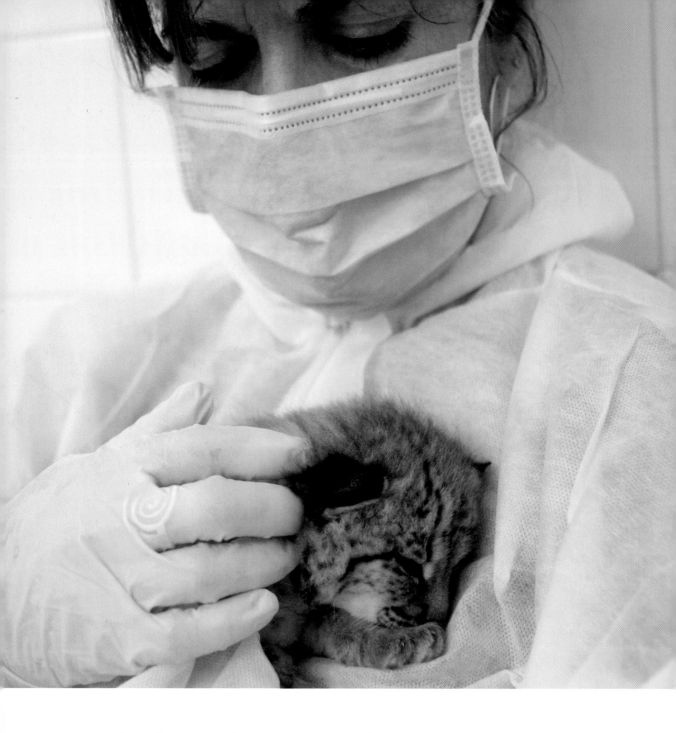

Cubs like a hug. And vets like to hug a cub.